Life Is Very Funny

David Walters

Copyright © David Walters 2024

All Rights Reserved

All rights reserved. No part of this publication may be reproduced, distributed, or transmitted in any form or by any means, including photocopying, recording, or other electronic or mechanical methods, without the author's prior written permission, except in the case of brief quotations embodied in critical reviews and certain other non-commercial uses permitted by copyright law. For permission requests, please get in touch with the author.

About the Author i

Forward ii

DOMESTIC BLISS 1

DAYS LIKE THIS 18

THE BIG WIDE WORLD 31

THE FACTS UNFURLED 46

DESPERATE MEASURES 65

OTHER PLEASURES 78

RHYME AND REASON 86

LOVE IN SEASON 102

A PICTURE OF HEALTH… 115

… AND OF WEALTH 133

SCIENTIFIC INVENTIONS 141

OTHER INTENTIONS 152

FANCY TRICKS 169

LIMERICKS 175

About the Author

David Walters was born in the East End of London in 1937. Despite humble beginnings he had a good education and qualified as an actuary. He became a merchant banker in the City of London and his work has taken him around the world. He has lived both in New York and California and visited many countries. He was married for over fifty years and has two children. Throughout his life his wry sense of humour has caused him to write lots of funny rhymes all of which are now collected in this book. He is retired but very active and lives in a retirement village in Hertfordshire.

Forward

I have always enjoyed playing with words and writing funny rhymes. Most of what I write is meant to be amusing but there are a few serious poems among the humorous ones. They are a wry look at life from my perspective. I hope that you enjoy them.

David Walters

January 2024

DOMESTIC BLISS

Non compute mentis

Of all the gadgets in my house

There's none astuter

Than my computer.

I use it for all sorts of things.

From playing games to e-mailing.

But strange to say –

There's no dispute –

I seldom use it

To compute.

Interior Decorating

Paint the woodwork,

Varnish the doors,

Paper the walls

And carpet the floors.

While all of this is quite rational

It's said to be old fashional.

So … varnish the woodwork,

Paper the doors,

Carpet the walls.

And paint the floors.

This may be seen as trendy.

But I think it's round-the-bendy.

Bedtime Prayer

I hope you have a very good night,

And wake up feeling fresh and bright,

But please, my darling, I implore,

Don't lie on your back and snore.

Grass

I sow it.

I grow it.

I mow it.

I throw it.

Party Boomer

When our neighbours have a party

It's always loud and hearty,

And I wouldn't want to stop them having fun.

But lying here in bed

With a pillow on my head

I just cannot wait until their party's done.

They always have a roomful,

And I'm sure the music's tuneful,

With lots of tasty snacks for them to eat,

But from here within my room

I can't hear a single tune,

Just the boom, boom, boom of the beat.

Not a Trifle

The custard's coloured purple,

The sponge is coloured green,

The jelly is of a sort

Which I have never seen.

The sherry isn't sherry

There's been a subtle change.

All in all, to sum it up,

It is a trifle strange.

A Dog's Life

According to my wife, our cat's

The master of our house.

Would somebody please tell her

I'm a man and not a mouse.

Forlorn Lawn

My lawn gives me

So much trouble

That it's now known as

Designer stubble.

Magnetic Attraction

Our kitchen looked bare -

Not lived in any more -

So we put all the magnets

Back on the fridge door.

Redundancy

It used to be the general case

To repair was cheaper than to replace;

But now it is by no means rare

To replace is cheaper than to repair.

Important article

I like my shirt crisp and neat.

I'm fastidious, I guess.

So iron with care and I'll wear

It hot off the press.

Tailored

My shirt has a tear.

Would you sew the seam?

It's an easy repair;

Or sew it would seam.

Continuous Loop

Put on my tie

Drink coffee down

Kiss wife goodbye

Commute into town

At desk all day

Make that last call

On motorway

A free-for-all

Clean up and eat

Hear the wife's views

Put up my feet

Watch TV news

And so to bed

It's sleep I crave

There's the alarm

Shower and shave

Put on my tie

Drink coffee down

Kiss wife goodbye

Commute into town ...

Unkind Cutter

When the lawn mower needed a service

I decided to do it myself.

I was not the least bit nervous

As I took my tools from the shelf.

I dismantled it with care

And cleaned up every part.

Reassembled it right there

And now the thing won't start.

End of the Line

We had a rotary clothesline

Installed in our back yard,

And there it stood so proudly

Like a soldier would, on guard.

We hung out all our washing

It never did complain.

The washing usually got dry

Unless there was some rain.

And then one day - disaster -

Some gismo in it lapsed

We looked out at our garden

And the clothesline had collapsed.

We all tried to revive it

But it was no longer young.

We think its problem was

That it got too highly strung.

And so our dear old clothes line

Has finally dropped dead,

And now we have replaced it

With a tumble drier instead.

Time Waster

When I buy a modern appliance,

Be it a fridge or electric wok,

It's certain that built in will be

A digital electric clock.

This fetish with chronometry

Is getting out of line

As it takes an hour to change the clocks

To daylight saving time.

False Alarm

Doorbells chime,

Telephones ring,

Alarms beep,

Microwaves ping;

Noises heard

Across the nation

Causing some

Aggravation.

As warning bells

They catch on fast

But as sound effects

In most broadcasts

They bring confusion

To every home;

"Is that the TV

Or the phone?"

Packaged Goods

To prise open a jar can be a pain,

But much worse is tightly wrapped
cellophane.

Childhood As It Used To Be

I'm not a baby.

I'm almost seven

And I can do things grown-ups can't.

I can crawl through holes

And climb big trees

And I can run very fast, but I shan't.

I like sweets;

Especially toffees

But mummy hides them away.

My best friend's William

I'm bigger than him

And he comes to our house to play.

I can read big words

And I can write

And I can add and take away.

I don't know why

I go to school

As there's not much to learn each day.

Grown-ups ask me

What I will be

When I grow up and I'm big.

I think that's silly

I won't tell them

'Cause I don't want to tell a fib.

But maybe I

Will learn to fly

Or ride a horse like cowboys do.

And stay up late

And say rude words

Which I am not allowed to do.

But mummy says

It's time for bed

And she always comes to tuck me in.

And daddy's going to

Read to me

A story called Rin Tin Tin.

Mummy says I must say goodnight.

Goodnight.

Proud Father

If I speak I must whisper quite soft

And I know that my head's in a whirl.

Who'd have thought that I'd be the father

Of a beautiful baby girl.

I can't speak without shouting out loud;

I can't smile without laughing for joy.

I'm chuffed, I'm ecstatic, I'm proud.

My wife's given birth to a boy.

DAYS LIKE THIS

The Mistake

Computation.

Disputation.

Altercation.

Arbitration.

Explanation.

Alteration.

Aggravation.

Compensation.

Look Alikes!

Last Sunday week

I went to see

A man who looked

A lot like me.

Now I'd not want

To drop a clanger

With someone who's

My doppelganger,

But I asked,

"How could it be

That you look

So much like me?"

"No, no," he said,

"This is not true.

You look like me,

Not me like you."

We argued thus

From dawn to dusk

Till both of us

Decided thus:

Don't make a fuss

We look like us

And let's both hope

That we don't see

Someone else

Who looks like we!

Sartorial Let Down

Smart business suit, crisp shirt, nice tie,

So it comes as quite a shock,

To see that as he walks away,

There's a large hole in his sock.

Use Your Head

You've put your foot in it, my friend,

The reason for which I'll explain.

It's because your foot is at the end

That's furthest from your brain.

Cockney Cutter

My barber's a cheerful bloke,

'Appy-go-lucky, never a care,

And when 'e's in 'is barber shop

'E's walking on 'air.

Timing

One of my true virtues

No one's ever there to see

Is that I arrive

Punctually.

English Weather

In winter, when we should be fitter,

The cold is bitter

But in summer it's the norm

For the bitter to be warm.

Patron Pending

Waiter, waiter, serving right,

Why am I out of your sight?

Though I try to catch your eye

You just keep on walking by.

Additional Comment

"The rain it raineth on the just

And also on the unjust fella:

But chiefly on the just, because

The unjust steals the just's umbrella."

One can't help feeling sorry for

The gentleman who penned this rhyme.

I always keep a spare in store,

He could have borrowed at the time.

(With apologies to Charles, Baron Bowen (1835-1874) who penned the first four lines.)

Poor View

Television is a time wasting trap

That, in my view, consists mostly of crap.

Perhaps that's why the younger generation

Has such a fertile imagination.

Indulgence

Oh, young Lochinvar has come out of the pub.

He's drunk too much beer without any grub.

He sways to the left, he sways to the right,

Don't dare call him drunk or you'll be in a fight.

He wanders around intending to find

A suitable place to park his behind

Whereupon his best mate comes to the pub door

And calls, "What ya doin'? Come and 'ave a few more."

And a few more he has, and so it goes on,

Another night drinking, another day gone.

Never ending

When you've reached the barrel's bottom

And you think your work is done,

Someone, just to be rotten,

Will open another one.

The Song of the Motorist

(To the tune of The Ash Grove)

By yonder parking meters

Traffic wardens do wander

Looking for vehicles

Whose time has run out.

They write them a ticket

On the windscreen they stick it

Then bugger off sharply

While no-ones about.

They walk away smugly

Before things turn ugly

Which occasionally happens

I have no doubt.

    Of traffic calming measures

    There are far too many

With sleeping policemen

Round-abouts and chicanes.

You can ruin your suspension

Or scrape the car badly

On posts that they put there

To stop trucks and cranes.

Yellow lines that are double

Get drivers in trouble

If they park their vehicles there

During the day.

It's not a surprise that

The police they don't buy that

So they order a tow truck

To tow them away.

The compounds in Peckham

And once you have got there

You won't like the charges

That you have to pay.

    Speed cameras we all hate

    On metal poles they lie in wait

    To photograph motorists

    Who inadvertently speed.

    Then two or three weeks later

    They get quite a shock

    When they open their post

    And their penalty read.

Petrol tax and vehicle excise

Are set at too big a size

Especially compared to

What foreigners pay.

And on motor insurance

They've added one more tax

And all us poor motorists

Just don't get a say.

But despite all these problems

We still drive our vehicles

'Cause none of us want

To use the railway.

THE BIG WIDE WORLD

Museum Guide

The waxworks on the first floor

Are stars of screen and stage.

The waxworks on the second floor

Are of a bygone age.

The waxworks on the third floor

Are horrible and gory.

I won't go into detail

As that's another storey.

Oh, England!

Oh, England, that I hate;

Your sprawling towns, your motorways,

Your pop generation with uncouth ways,

Your winters damp that chill the bone

Incessant chatter on mobile phone

Graffiti scrawled on railway walls

The supermarket child that bawls

Cheap council housing, now a slum,

Pavements marked with well-chewed gum,

Beer cans parked on any ledge

How it puts my nerves on edge.

Oh, England, that I love;

Your rolling hills and craggy shores

Your villages with village stores

Your leafy glades and country lanes

Thatched cottages with weathervanes.

Your pubs with ancient beams and walls

Your stately homes with splendid halls

Your history and pageantry

Your freedom and democracy

Your quaint traditions and quirky ways

I would not change in a million days.

North, South, East or West

When flying out of London

I'm confused not in the least.

To America I fly west

To the Far East I fly east.

But what I do find worrying

Whenever I sally forth

Is, whether I'm going east or west,

I start by flying north.

The Business Traveller's Ode

When I'm stuck in a hotel room

And retire for the night

It's nice to have across the room

The TV's stand-by light.

And should I wake, as I sometimes do,

In the middle of the night,

What guides me to the bathroom

Is the TV's stand-by light.

It's there when I leave in the morning;

It's there when I'm back at night.

A little ray of comfort is

The TV's stand-by light.

And up and down the country

In hotels left and right

It's nice to know that in each room

Is the TV's stand-by light.

Map Reader

I'm not one who likes to travel,

The efforts not worth the reward

But give me a map to unravel

And for sure I'll not be bored.

Those mountains, rivers, cities, shores,

The exotic places I've found;

Thus my imagination soars

But my feet stay on the ground.

Moving Verse

While travelling by plane

I'm rhyming a notion.

Is this what they call

Poetry in motion?

The Shipping Forecast

Here is the shipping forecast for O-six hundred hours.

The general synopsis, moderate wind, occasional showers.

Viking and North Utsire, winds veering west

Winds variable 4 or 5 increasing 6 at best.

South Utsire, northeast Forties, Cromarty and Forth

Winds variable, 3 or 4 veering to the north.

Southwest Forties, Tyne, Dogger, Fisher, German Bight

Visibility poor, rain later, seas moderate to light.

Wight, Humber, Thames, Dover, Portland, Plymouth, Biscay

Winds west 3 or 4; smooth or slight throughout the day.

Southeast Fitzroy, Northwest Fitzroy, Sole, Lundy, Fastnet

North or northeast 3 or 4, becoming variable and wet.

Irish Sea, Shannon, Rockall, Malin, Hebrides

West or southwest 6 or 7, rough or very rough seas.

Bailey, Faeroes, Southeast Iceland and finally Fair Isle

Winds 4 or 5, rain or squally showers for a while.

This ends the shipping forecast from the BBC.

We wish you safe sailing while you are at sea.

I Rest My Case

When the plane stops at the gate

The rush to leave I know well,

So that we can wait

At the luggage carousel.

Foreign Exchange

It's fun to visit foreign places -

To see new sights - to meet new faces,

But currency, I find, frustrates me

The exchange rate always moves against me.

Going Up

Elevators boast

To move people the most.

Thus more of us ride

Up and down than side to side.

Incident at St. Peter's

I stand in the rain and cough and wheeze

To see his holiness, I hope.

He comes to the balcony. I sneeze.

"Bless you," says the Pope.

Traveller's Lament

Map makers are devilish clever

And to them I raise my cap.

How do they put each place I want

In the fold of every map?

Free to Travel

Stand up and be counted.

Get your picture taken and mounted.

And for being a good sport

Here's your new passport.

Ski Holiday

Up the mountain, ride;

Down the mountain, fall.

Broken bones, plaster cast;

Bye, regards to all.

Happy Intersections

Here's a thought on which to chew

Traffic lights are never blue!

Expanding Girth

Why is a muffin English?

Why are French fries French?

Why is an omelette Spanish?

Is all this making sense?

Food is international,

Its origins keep me guessing;

Was it the Italians

Who made that salad dressing?

I much prefer home cooking

For me it hit's the spot,

But I concede my stomach

Has travelled an awful lot.

Nationality

When someone asks me where I'm from,

When I travel abroad from here,

I pause before I answer

As it isn't very clear.

I'm English, that I know for sure,

And British too; that's rational.

But I also live in the UK

Which makes me a UK national.

England, Wales and Scotland

Are Great Britain when combined,

Add in Northern Ireland

And it's the UK you've defined.

So why do we confuse ourselves.

With a country that complicates?

No other country does it,

Not even the United States.

Speeding

Oh, it's great to be on the open road.

What a lucky fellow I am.

I can't wait to put my foot down

Once I'm through this traffic jam.

THE FACTS UNFURLED

Change of weapon

Who lives by the sword dies by the sword.

Thus endeth lesson one.

But you should know,

That the facts clearly show

Who lives by the sword dies by the gun.

Mary

Mary had a little lamb -

A fact well known, of course.

But on the occasion to which I refer

She had it with mint sauce.

Listen Here

"Unaccustomed as I am to public speaking..."

Is an excuse that a speaker will sometimes plead.

As a member of the public who must listen,

I am very accustomed to public speaking indeed.

Name the Decade

In the twenties and the thirties

Boom and bust were almost certain.

In the forties and the fifties

World War II and Iron Curtain.

In the sixties and the seventies

Rock and roll and Vietnam.

In the eighties and the nineties

Communism proved a sham.

In the new millennium,

Global warming and jihad.

Are things any better

Or are they just as bad?

The years rush by

Each decade goes

And what comes next

No-one knows.

Back in the USSR

There's Kirgizstan, Tajikistan,
Turkmenistan, Uzbekistan

Latvia, Lithuania, Estonia and Kazakhstan,

Belorussia, Moldova, Armenia, Azerbaijan,

Georgia, Ukraine and Russia add up to
fifteen, by darn!

I'm trying to remember all these new names
that are on the map

I don't think that my memory can really
cope with names like that.

I know that I will mix them up and never
work out where they are.

It all was so much easier when it was just
USSR.

Rocks

The behaviour of rocks is very strange,

Though easy to forecast.

Either they stay very, very still

Or whiz past very fast.

Population Explosion

There is no dearth

Of life on Mother Earth.

In fact, if you measure 'er

You'll find that there's a plethora.

Sausages

Sausages are very fryable

A fact easily verifiable.

Weather Report

The weather's turned quite awful

With gale force winds, you know,

And if you've got a minute

I'll describe it blow by blow.

Newspeak

Broadcasters on radio and TV choose

An impartial manner to present the news;

Not conversational in tone

Or as you might sound on the phone,

But measured, precise, without emotion,

The flow of words like a soothing lotion.

If we all chose to speak like that

Conversation would sound extremely flat.

Cucumbers

Of vegetables there are any number,

But none quite like the green cucumber.

If you never cooked or had advice

You might think it grew slice by slice.

Uncertainty

Absence makes the heart grow fonder:

Absence leaves the heart to wander.

Here's a source of confusion;

Same start but different conclusion

Which proves, I suppose, for all to see

The principle of uncertainty.

Turn Off

I do not wear pyjamas.

The reason is, dear sir,

When I turn over in my bed

The pants stay where they were!

Case Proven?

Upon discussion we concluded,

The art of conversation's dead

As is the art of reading books -

According to a book I read.

Improssable

If something is possible

It means that it might be

And if it is probable

It's more than likely.

But this, I think,

You will have to agree,

While the improbable is possible

The impossible cannot be.

Name Dropper

What's in a name,

I hear you exclaim.

I'll tell you without any fuss.

It really is vital

We each have a title

So that I can tell you from us.

Latin Scholar

I like to use i.e.

I like to use e.g.

And when circumstances permit

I show off a bit

With q.e.d.

Cliché Update

From little acorns, so they say,

Mighty oak trees grow

But who can wait that long?

The process is too slow.

Pouring oil on troubled waters

Used to be recommended,

But now environmentalists

Want the practice ended.

Putting the cart before the horse,

Has merit, may I remind you;

For, without meaning to be coarse,

The horse's rear's behind you.

The Year

Winter freezes.

Spring breezes.

Summer's hot.

Autumn's not.

Timely Remark

She has an hourglass figure,

The envy of the stout,

But between you and me

The sand is running out.

Meaning

Who called it a "Dictionary" took

An old-style meaning for the book.

It would have been more visionary

To have called it the "Definitionary".

Wear and Tear

Age and gravity take their toll

As the years go by,

And soon you need extra support

From the underwear you buy.

Politically Correct

Don't say "mail",

It could be misheard

Better say "post"

A more neutral word.

Likewise "made"

Could be confused;

We recommend "produced"

Should be used.

And one more thing

We must bar,

Don't laugh "he-he-he"

Better use "ha-ha-ha".

Lottery

Pick your numbers carefully,

But whichever one's you choose,

Sometimes you'll win,

Most times you'll lose.

Seeing the Light

I had a difficult problem

Not easy to solve in the least.

Does the sun rise in the west

Or does the sun rise in the east?

I lay awake all night thinking

The idea of sleep I scorned.

And then as the morning approached,

The answer upon me dawned.

Sized Up

It used to be, I recall,

Things I bought

Were large or small.

Now I note, with no pleasure,

That things I buy

Are micro or mega.

Stretching the truth

There's no point in asking the question,

You'll only be misled.

Don't expect a truthful answer

From someone lying in bed.

Modern Times

Everyone knows

That the sun rose

At dawn this morning

And it's an easy bet

That the sun will set

At last light tonight.

What complicates this tranquil scene

Is what will happen in-between.

Learning Curve

When I was a mite

I knew not what,

And life was simple

From my baby's cot.

When I was a lad

I knew it all

The path was clear,

No place to fall.

When I was a man

With a lot to learn,

What I didn't know

Gave me cause for concern.

Now as the years

Accelerate by

I know what I know

To the rest, goodbye!

Career Path

Education's a wonderful thing

So let's have more of it, please

If you want to reach the top

You can do so by degrees.

DESPERATE MEASURES

There's a Space for Us

A collision with an asteroid

Is something that we must avoid;

And to make the point succinct

The dinosaurs didn't and they're extinct.

Cockroach

Five cars, two trucks and a coach

Ran over a large cockroach.

There's a dent in the road where the cockroach lay,

But it got up and walked away.

Bad Night

I've been awake since half-past-two;

Walked around, been to the loo;

Made myself a cup of tea,

Watched an old movie on TV,

And now with dawn about to break

I'm back in bed but still awake;

Then finally I drink sleep's cup

And the bloody alarm wakes me up.

Ticklish Business

The tickle that's the worst -

There's nothing that can match it -

Is the one inside your ear,

And there's no way you can scratch it.

Bad Business

Industrial dispute

Withdrawal of labour

Peaceful picketing

Striking behaviour

Loss of production

Sales take a dent

And all because of

One per cent.

Book Critic

The book I take from the rack

Presents me with a riddle.

Why is it a "paper back"

And not "paper front" or "middle"?

Competition Junkie

I enter newspaper competitions

I can't count how many I've lost.

Now I need to win a major prize

Just to cover my mailing cost.

Night in the City

At night I lie in bed

And listen to the hush

As footsteps cease their tread

And cars no longer rush.

And I wonder if I care,

Should anyone find it queer,

That we rush from here to there

And back from there to here.

And so I fall asleep

And awaken near the dawn

Not from my alarm's bleep

But some idiot's car horn.

Flagged Down

He was a maker of flags,

(His firm were once my tenants)

But he made a mistake with the Union Jack

Since which time he does pennants.

Fare's Fair

I can't see what the fuss is

About the London busses

They get you there eventually.

So I'm told.

The trains that go by rail

Hardly ever fail,

Except for a few new ones

And the old.

The London Underground

Is basically sound

Apart from escalators -

Tunnels - trains.

They all work fairly well,

So I have heard tell,

Unless the weather's sunny

Or it rains.

So office girl

And city gent

Please pay your fare,

It's cash well spent.

You may get there

Crowded and cramped

But it must be better

Than being clamped.

Tough Choice

So many products now I find

Give a date to use by,

But if I'm to get out of the store

I need a date to choose by.

Swear Off

One used to need some unction

To describe a bodily function

In a manner that was open and was frank

But now you don't need daring,

Why, everyone is swearing,

If you object, you're thought of as a crank.

Most letters of the alphabet

Now describe another set

Of words that I consider very rude

But don't use the initial,

It's OK and official

To shout them out, even if they're crude.

On the advice of the constabulary

I limit my vocabulary

Avoiding the shocking and profane.

I suppose that I may bore us

With words from my thesaurus

But the sensitive among us don't complain.

Enfant Terrible

Terrible child,

Spoilt and precocious,

Running wild,

Manners atrocious.

Why, dear Lord,

Must it be

That they always

Sit next to me?

Holey Mess

Too many people that I know

Who have troubles by the score,

Don't try to get out of the hole they're in.

They just dig a little bit more.

Web of Intrigue

In order to eavesdrop

Some people make the call

That they would like to be

A fly upon the wall.

When I hear this wish

I'm tempted to reply

That I would like to be

A spider nearby.

Unwanted Attention

I'm quiet - not one to make a display.

Loud people leave me ill at ease.

Yet everyone turns to look my way

At the noise I make when I sneeze.

Haunted

Ghosts and spirits,

Wraiths and ghouls;

Unearthly noises

Deep in the night;

But they are nothing,

They make us fools;

It's the plumbing

That isn't right.

More, Please

Life isn't very easy,

In fact it's rough and tough,

But, I think, for most of us

We cannot get enough.

Death isn't very easy

And it is forever,

But, I think, for most of us

We'd rather it were never.

OTHER PLEASURES

Eating Out

Sitting at their tables

Waiting to be served

The patrons look around

Observing and observed;

But, of greater interest

Than casual observation,

Is to listen surreptitiously to

The next table's conversation.

Fashion Statement

Those handsome guys and gals

On the catwalk slowly go.

Now that is what I call

A model portfolio.

Decline a Recliner

Most chairs I am happy to sit on

They're relaxing and have some appeal

But three I wish to avoid

Are the dentist, electric and wheel.

Sweet Tooth

When choosing breakfast cereal

My confusion is often noted.

Should I have the sugar frosted

Or, instead, the honey coated?

Bath Time

Some like to wash in a shower,

Some into a bath will flop,

One makes you wet from top to bottom,

The other from bottom to top.

Oops!

I sat in the lap of luxury

Drinking from its cup.

All was fine and dandy

Then luxury stood up.

Cheer up

Life is full of ups and downs,

Not every day is sunny,

But smiles outnumber tears and frowns.

Now don't you think that's funny?

Lunch order

Give me a cheese and pickle sandwich,

The kind you make the best,

Where the cheese is very cheesy

And the pickle's full of zest

Between two slices of the finest

Bread there is in town

And a large mug of coffee

To help the food go down

Breakfast

Strong, hot coffee in a large cup,

Cereal, toast and then

Two or three eggs fried sunny side up -

My compliments to the hen.

Pop-up Book

When I was young I learnt about

How people dress and cook

By looking at the pictures

In my little pop-up book.

And dinosaurs and monsters,

I found out how they look

From all the scary pictures

In my little pop-up book.

But when it came to sex

I discovered what it took,

And what popped-up wasn't in

My little pop-up book.

Diminuendo

I went to a concert.

It was very mean.

Just a piano

And a tambourine.

I went to another.

It was even meaner.

All they had

Was a concertina.

I went to a third.

It was the meaniest.

No instruments at all,

Not even the teeniest.

Bargain Hunter

At sale time I fly

To the shopping mall,

But the things I buy

Aren't in the sale at all.

Retribution

I like to eat dinner out,

Of that there is no question

But afterwards, there is no doubt,

I'll suffer indigestion.

RHYME AND REASON

Paging FJ

Frère Jacques,

Frère Jacques,

Call for you.

Call for you.

Pick it up on line two.

Pick it up on line two.

Putting you through.

Putting you through.

Old Age

I've been around for many years,

More than I'd care to mention,

And now that I know all the answers

Nobody asks me a question.

Ultimatum

The next line of this verse

Is the antepenultimate one.

My penultimate line is terse

And my ultimate line is done.

Animation

Lambs don't drive Lamborghinis

Or a cat sail a catamaran,

Rats don't eat ratatouille,

Though I have no doubt they can.

Bulls don't bite the bullet,

And stags don't often stagger,

Ants don't use antacid

And I know of no nag that's a nagger.

Hens don't hire henchman

And cows are seldom cowardly

Dogs don't write this doggerel

As that's what I do, avowedly.

Word Processor

A poet is an artist of magnificent words and sounds

With stanzas of great beauty where imagery abounds.

I'm no poet -

I'm much worse.

I just write

Terse verse.

Etc.

I use this little word

When I want to show

That I know more

Than I know.

Last Laugh

I have a sense of humour

Of that there is no doubt.

I laugh at many a bloomer

I know what a joke's about.

But don't ask me to tell one,

For that I'm hopeless doin'.

I know how it should be done,

But it's the last line that I ruin.

There, There

"Their", "they're" and "there" are

Three words over which I glitch,

For when I go to write them

I mix up which is which.

Poetic Justice

This is the tale of a very bad poet

Who didn't want the world to know it.

He concocted lies and extravaganzas

That thieves had stolen his rhymes and stanzas.

The cops were called to look into the crime

They read all his doggerel - examined each rhyme -

And discovered the fraud. So without much reticence,

They confiscated his poetic license.

To My Fellow Rhymesters

To all my fellow rhymesters

I offer you this thought:

While in our mind each line stirs

To get the meaning caught,

The genuine satisfaction

Which we seek every time

Is neat word interaction

To make the damn thing rhyme.

Modern poetry

Is it a poem or is it prose?

Seems to me that anything goes

So long as it has a beat

But rhyming it would be too neat.

And then the ideas that they write

Are far too clever - even trite.

Why do I need to wrack my brain

To understand what should be plain?

I think I'll stick to Keats and Shelley

Or better still, go watch the tele!

A Word in Your Ear

There are some words, when I write,

For which I like to make room,

Like "wherewithal" and "heretofore"

And "midst" and "thus" and "whom".

Recording!

In philosophical mood I ponder life's order

And note that it's like a video recorder.

As a child, time goes slowly from day-to-day

And one naturally presses the button marked "play".

An adult work's hard to earn just reward.

Time goes quickly with the button marked "fast forward".

Should we fall ill for any cause,

Then we should use the button marked "pause".

We retire with memories filling our mind

Which we play back often with the button "rewind".

And when we reach the end of the tape

We are stored in a box of appropriate shape.

Punch Line

A few words to set the scene;

A few more to expand the theme;

Build it up with impressive facts,

And close with an anti-climax.

Give a Little Whistle

When I was a lad my friends and me

Would whistle while Crosby would croon,

And on the wireless there'd always be

Someone who'd whistle a tune.

But people don't whistle so much today,

As an art they seem to ignore it

Back then it made us happy and gay

But now you can whistle for it.

Waning lyrical

Where are the songs of yesteryear

The one's with a lyric and tune,

The one's that Frank Sinatra

And Bing Crosby used to croon?

Where are the songs of yesteryear

The ones I know so well?

New music that I hear

Just doesn't ring that bell.

Where are the songs of yesteryear

Sung in bars, dark and smoky?

Ah yes, I think I've found them.

They're at the karaoke.

Off Beat?

While it may seem rude to some

To use words like "titty" and "bum"

The context is to help this ditty

Go bum-titty-bum-titty-bum-bum-titty.

Word Play

According to Wilfred Funk the 10 most beautiful words in the English language are: dawn, lullaby, hush, luminous, murmuring, tranquil, mist, chimes, golden and melody. (I have also heard it argued that "cellar door" is the most beautiful!). Thus I would suggest:

The golden melody of tranquil dawn

Murmuring in the luminous mist

The lullaby's chimes are hushed and gone

The cellar door by sunlight kissed.

According to The National Association of Teachers of Speech the 10 ugliest words are: phlegmatic, crunch, flatulent, cacophony, treachery, sap, jazz, plutocrat, gripe and plump. Thus:

Plump plutocrat, I'm not a sap.

Your jazzy cacophony

Of treachery, gripe and crunch

Leaves me phlegmatic.

I ignore the crap

Of your flatulent spouting after lunch.

Makes Sense

We all know our five senses well;

There's taste and touch, sound, sight and smell.

But there are five others, I would say,

Just as important in their way.

Our sense of justice, our sense of beauty,

Our sense of order, our sense of duty

And, perhaps I should have mentioned sooner,

Our all-important sense of humour.

Immortalised in Rhyme

Many a clever quip or pun

Is soon forgotten by everyone,

But those that stand the test of time

Often do so because they rhyme.

LOVE IN SEASON

Macedoine of Veg

Said the parsnip to the swede, who had bean for a pea,

"You look so radishing, will you marrow me?

Lettuce beetroot in holy onion wed.

Here's a ten-carrot ring to wear on your head."

Latest Liaison

This electric passion

The two of us share

Must be what they call

A current affair.

The Aim of Love

When Cupid shoots his loving dart

To help along those hugs and kisses,

Am I right to assume

A miss is preferred to a mrs.?

Trouble on the Way

Their relationship's a mess.

The problem's quite acute.

She's got a maternity dress.

He's got a paternity suit.

Shmotchky-Potchkela

My darling Shmotchky-Potchkela

My world is so hotch-potchkela

I yearn for you so muchkela,

I tingle to your touchkela.

That day when we had lunchkela

You called me honey-bunchkela,

But in English, French or Scotchkela

You are my Shmotchky-Potchkela.

Striptease

He took off her coat

Placed it on the chair.

Unbuttoned her blouse

And draped it there.

Unzipped her skirt

Hung it by the door.

Removed her shoes

Left them on the floor.

Here I draw a veil -

Let the matter close -

But he did look cute

In his mother's clothes.

Dan, Dan

(Written as a sequel to the anonymous poem:

Flo, Flo, I love you so

I love you in your nighty.

When moonlight flits across your tits

Jesus Christ Almighty.)

Dan, Dan, you are my man

With hairy back and chest.

Your muscles bulge - come, let's indulge,

And then we'll have a rest.

False Modesty?

I may look at x-rays of your torso

I may look at pictures of you dressed

But pictures in the nude

You don't want to be viewed.

This logic leaves me unimpressed.

A Homily About an Anomaly

"Seeking friendship" ads display for me and you

The virtues of lonely girls and guys

But, if what they say about themselves is true,

Why do they need to advertise?

Divorce Settlement

"'Tis better to have loved and lost …"

So the old saying ordained.

Methinks that it is better still

To have loved and gained.

Romantic Thinker

I'm quite a Romeo,

A real Casanova;

My conquests are many,

It's high turnover.

But no cause for concern

I think you'll find,

As all my conquests

Are in my mind.

One Night Stand

Oh say can you see

By the dawn's early light

Where I put my pants

I had on last night?

They're not on the banister,

They're not by the bed

Please get me two aspirin

To clear up my head.

The Rise and Fall of Male Virility

When I was a child I couldn't keep still

And my interest in girls was nil.

As an adolescent with hormones loaded

My interest in girls exploded.

When I reached the prime of life

I settled down with a lovely wife.

But I find old age somewhat hateful;

If my wife says "no" I'm extremely grateful.

Equals Repel

She's vivacious, audacious, flirtatious.

He's charming, disarming, alarming.

When they meet … oh brother!

They can't bear each other.

The Golfer (for Anna)

There is a young lady who I adore.

She suits me to a tee.

I don't think I could ask for more

Than having her with me.

She always scores an easy par

And sets my heart a-flutter

To see her I will travel far

With or without my putter.

Love You Down to Your Little Cotton Socks

You're no star in a blockbuster movie;

You're not the lead in a Broadway play;

But you always were and will be

The one I love today.

I know you're no TV idol

Or a champ at any sport,

But for me you have no rival;

I love you and I'm caught.

And although I don't say this often

And you may get kind of sore,

Though I love you very dearly,

Pick your socks up off the floor.

A poem of love

I love your nose

I love your toes

I love your arms

I love your charms

I love each thumb

I love your tum

I love your eyes

I love your thighs

My poems of love, I hope, are clear

I hope that you have got 'em.

So let me whisper in your

I love you from top to bottom.

The Star

There is a star that brightly shines

Many lifetimes away from here,

And sometimes at night

When the sky is clear

I gaze upon its tiny light

And wonder if around that star

There are two people like us

Who laugh and love

And gaze above

At the distant light from our sun at dusk.

And if they are there

I hope that they

Are as much in love as we are today.

A PICTURE OF HEALTH…

Growing old

As I've grown old I sleep less well,

As any early bird can tell.

As I've grown old I take more pills

And creams and lotions for my ills.

As I've grown old I'm walking slower

And parts of me are hanging lower.

As I've grown old I've developed a tum

And cellulite dimples on my bum.

As I've grown old my libido's waned

And both my legs are varicose veined.

But growing old I can forgive,

It's better than the alternative.

Salt and Pepper

Whether it's meat,

Whether it's fish,

Salt and pepper

Enhance the dish.

But please take care,

Don't overdo it,

For if you do

You'll surely rue it.

Sad Story

Daphne fell ill.

Then she felt better

Whereupon

Henrietta ...

Growing Pains

When I was five we'd mark the wall

To see if I was growing tall

At fifteen I would celebrate

To note my chest's expanding state

But now I'm old, it is perverse,

Any change is for the worse.

Picture Story

As I lie on the hospital bed

While pictures of my inside are created,

I wonder, will I get to see them,

Or will they be X-rayted?

Relief

Each day I wake -

Get out of bed

It's nice to know

That I'm not dead.

Organist

As a transplant surgeon he specialised

In livers, kidneys and hearts.

I suppose that you could call him

A man of many parts.

Hypochondriac

It seems I must be more discreet

When talking about my new disease,

As many doctors that I meet

Turn out to be just PhD's.

Insomniac

Dear Aunt Daisy was terribly lazy -

Used to sleep all day in bed.

Then her physician

Cured her condition.

Now she lies awake instead.

Environmental Epitaph

When I was alive

Pollution I made.

Now that I'm dead

I biodegrade.

Meal Timing

When it comes to fasting

There's one thing I'd like to know

As it's called a fast

Why does it seem so slow?

And So To Bed

A cough, a chill, an ache, a snuffle,

One's equilibrium can ruffle,

Because each symptom portends a

Nasty case of influenza.

Inside Story

She agreed to an operation

After many ifs and buts.

The surgeon examined her x-ray

And said, "She's got guts!"

Positive Advice

If you can treat your tumour

With a sense of humour,

The carcinoma might

Just give up the fight.

Hospital Drama

The doctor looked at his notes -

Shook his head in some dismay.

The prognosis was not good

For the patient brought in that day.

His illnesses were many

And none of them were nice -

Syphilis, gonorrhoea, herpes

And HIV positive - twice!

But how to break the news

Without driving the poor guy frantic?

He walked over to his bed and said,

"You're an incurable romantic."

Thoughts in the Lavatory

How inelegant is diarrhoea.

You sit on the pot and you feel quite queer.

You have a stomach-ache so rare,

A strange aroma fills the air,

And when, at last, you think you've finished

It starts again, quite undiminished.

But then at last you're off the pot

And you begin to wipe your bot.

"My God," you say, "this is no laugh,

I think I need a bloomin' bath."

Uncontrolled Growth

Mind over matter is a goal to which we should strive

But the matter over my mind, that is the hair on my head,

Seems to have lost the will to survive.

In the meantime, it happily sprouts elsewhere, wouldn't you know,

Growing in my ears, nostrils and other places

Where I don't want it to grow.

You Should Live So Long

(News Item - Doctors have discovered that one's ears grow throughout life at the rate of about one tenth of a millimetre each year.)

When I have good news to divest

My family say they're all ears.

Calculations now suggest

They will be in ten thousand years.

Clean Machine

About personal hygiene I am meticulous,

Washing and scrubbing to a degree quite ridiculous

Trimming the nails on my fingers and toes,

And carefully removing the hairs from my nose.

Fatty

I have a dream,

Call it a whim -

To eat what I like

And yet stay slim.

Unsportsmanlike

My wife and I are middle aged

Not active in any sport

We mainly get our exercise

From gardening or a walk.

But in spite of this evidence

Which I have clearly put,

She has tennis elbow

And I have athlete's foot.

Cold Feet

You may suffer cold feet when about to perform

On stage or on TV.

You may suffer cold feet when you need a job

And you're the interviewee.

You may suffer cold feet in the waiting room

When the dentist calls for you.

You may suffer cold feet at the altar

When your bridegroom says, "I do".

You may suffer cold feet in time of war

With a dangerous mission ahead

But the cold feet that I suffer

Are the one's my wife brings to bed.

Getting Through It

When you've got cancer, a malignant tumour,

It doesn't put you in a good humour

And the resultant chemotherapy

Is something you'd rather never see.

But having been put through the mill

Of hospital visits and pill after pill,

When you emerge from all that stuff,

Even though it has been quite rough,

You may be hairless

But you couldn't care less.

If when it is over, you are assured

That, yes, you really have been cured.

Figure it out? Not me!

Thank goodness for the business suit

That fits neatly over my torso

Hiding from all those I meet

Where I bulge, not a little, but more so.

Laxative

A lot of nervous anticipation

Is sure to cure constipation.

Forty Something

Age forty-one, I conclude,

Precedes the age of fortitude.

Alphabetic Ailment

Anytime, anywhere

Being old, breathing air.

Catch a cold, catch a chill

Damp draughts, feeling ill.

Easy does it, easy there,

Fight the flu. It's not fair.

Get a gargle, go to bed.

Have an ache in my head.

I'll be OK by tomorrow

Just let me wallow in my sorrow.

Kind of you to offer aid

Leave me be, just draw the shade.

Make a cup of herbal tea,

Not too hot to bother me.

Oh doesn't this get on your wick?

People hate it when you're sick.

Quiet is all I need.

Rotten cold! Can't even read.

Sneezing, coughing, watery eyes

Tissues galore by my side.

Up in the dead of night

Very ill and what a sight.

What a sight, I'm almost dead.

Xylophone banging in my head!

Yawn I think I'm feeling sleepy,

Zzzzzzzz …

... AND OF WEALTH

Investor Dilemma

To buy stocks and shares is easy,

As we all know well,

But it is so much harder

To know when to sell.

Long-Term Investor

Stock exchange fashions come and go.

I'm an investor - I ought to know.

My share holdings now consist

Of stocks once on the fashion list.

By this means I have acquired

A balanced portfolio - much admired.

Financial Fun

It's fairly easy to be funny

In rhymes about investing money.

It's much more difficult to be comical

About the economy and things economical.

Advice to Risk Takers

A company's profit forecast

Should be treated with trepidation,

For experience suggests achievement

Is the square root of expectation.

The Investor's Rap

I had a little money that I wanted to invest

So I called my friendly broker and I asked him what was best.

He said, "I've got a stock that I strongly recommend.

Its earnings will be higher with a big fat dividend."

I bought a lot of shares and the earnings were announced.

The market didn't like them and the price was badly trounced.

So I called my friendly broker and I asked him what to do

He said, "Don't worry, Dave, I've a better stock for you."

I switched into the new shares and they were getting warm;

They had a new invention that would take the world by storm.

But all their money went and they could get no more,

The market didn't like it and the price dropped through the floor.

So I dumped my friendly broker and I realised my loss.

I thought I'd make some money but now I'm very cross.

I walked into a little bank and put my money there

And it has now gone belly up, so all I've got is air.

Cut the Hedge

According to my investment guru

I should be using hedges

But a hedge is difficult to see through

And fuzzy around the edges.

I'm the cautious kind

As you can tell

I don't want to lose my shirts.

When you fall on a hedge

As I know full well

It gives no support - and it hurts.

Dress Code

Stock and bond traders,

Security vendors,

Corporate raiders,

Financial contenders

All identified

By their red suspenders.

Poor People

Fortune favours the brave,

Of that I have no doubt

But looking at those around me

There are a lot of cowards about.

Market Tracker

Stock prices rise

I'm feeling brave.

I'm fully invested

To ride the wave.

Stock prices fall;

I don't want to sell.

I'm fully invested.

Oh, what the hell.

Looking Up

I have the impression

There's been a recession,

As all of you will know.

It's very depressing

When things are recessing

And the economy goes slow.

But growth will follow

As spring does the swallow

Cheer up - it's just a blip.

The current ballistics

Of economic statistics

Don't make a double dip.

SCIENTIFIC INVENTIONS

You Have Mail

Oh, what a tangled web we weave

When first we practice to receive

E-mails that electronically jet

Across the ubiquitous Internet.

Technical Interface

Between fiction and fact

There is a disparity

Eliminated by

Virtual reality.

Netted and Hooked

I cannot swim;

I hate to shop;

But I surf the Net

Until I drop.

New Slant

I have an unusual question

Not in the maths curricula.

When a line meets a plane at an angle,

Is it perpenzontal or horindicular?

Is Anyone Out There?

In the search for intelligent life

There may prove to be a dearth,

But I sometimes think we should search

For intelligent life on Earth.

Noise Annoys

There are many inventions

With which the world is cursed,

But there is one

That I think is the worst.

It invades my privacy and makes my hearing weaker

I refer, of course, to the ubiquitous loudspeaker.

Colour Supplement

The rainbow's hues

Stretch from reds to blues

But missing, I think,

Are brown, mauve and pink

Mix and Match

Scientists have proven

A fact I find distracting

When we fall in love

It's just chemicals reacting.

I console myself however

At their lack of sensitivity

In the knowledge that their thinking's

Just electrical activity.

Big Cheese

(*News item - An astronomer has suggested that the missing matter in the universe is accounted for by billions of black holes*)

The wonder of the universe unrolls

It seems that it's now full of holes.

This news, I find, does not please

Who wants to live in a Swiss cheese?

Star Gazing

My small telescope

Can hardly cope,

But it's no trouble

With the Hubble.

Strange Turn of Events

I boarded a flight

Flying faster than light.

Before we took off we had landed.

Jet lag I exchanged

For something more strange,

As now I'm no longer right-handed.

Help

My new software has on-screen support

And I would not refuse it

But the help menu is so complex

That I need some help to use it.

Matter of Faith

In the universe, in every direction,

God's laws apply without exception

But if chance rules at the quantum level,

Perhaps it's because it's run by the Devil.

Diminishing Returns

Specialisation can be useful.

It keeps your eye on the ball

But at the extreme, you're a specialist

In what amounts to nothing at all!

Material Slip

(News item: A cloth containing Teflon has been developed that cannot be stained)

I'm pleased with my Teflon trousers,

My Teflon tie and shirt.

They can't be stained and repel

All grease and grime and dirt.

But there is one thing about them

Which worries me a bit

That is, I'm slipping and sliding

Everywhere I sit.

Auto Suggestion

(News item - Cars and pedestrians are more visible at night in ultra-violet light.)

Ford and GM

Have started a pilot

To paint their cars

In ultra-violet.

In ultra-violet

I'll not be seen dead

I want my car

In infra-red.

Inspiration

A brilliant idea once entered my mind;

An idea so clear and well defined

That I was sure it must have occurred

To each and every guru and nerd.

And so I worked at a feverish pace

Before all the others entered the race,

Only to discover the idea was flawed.

Oh, well! Back to the drawing board.

The Universe

The universe is a very strange place

Mainly composed of lots of space.

When it started it was so small.

That there was nothing there at all.

How it will end is quite a tease.

Answers on a postcard, please.

OTHER INTENTIONS

Political Prisoner

Talk of war

We abhor.

Practising anarchy

Makes us panicky.

We don't want theocracy,

We're a democracy.

And be advised

You're disenfranchised.

Country Scene

The cows are in the meadow

Eating of the grass,

Passing it through the other end,

Tread careful when you pass.

Hair Raising

Who can count

The hours she took

Just to create

The natural look.

Summit Conclusion

They've had their summit meeting.

I'll try to sum it up.

Some talked while they were eating,

Some over glass or cup.

To summarise the outcome

Of this important forum,

They'll meet again tomorrow

If they can get a quorum.

The Long Farewell

When visiting a friend or relation,

And we have our coats on to go,

I know the parting conversation

Will take another ten minutes or so.

Second Thoughts

As a democratic society

One's opinions are often voted,

And our leadership's variety

Has frequently been noted.

But what worries me, I fear,

Is, whoever we've selected,

It's quite clear within a year

We are sorry we elected.

Extremities

When you give someone a hand,

They greet it with a smile.

When you give someone a foot,

They often take a mile.

Hands applaud; hands are with it.

Feet stamp; don't put them in it.

Hands are OK; they're definitely in;

But poor old feet are out on a limb.

Places Names and Face Names

Places used to be named after people,

But there are few places now left to name.

So the tradition has been turned on its head,

And people are named after places instead

Art Critic

Modern art museums

I view with some alarm.

Most exhibits that they show

Are lacking any charm.

I admit that they are colourful

And clever in design,

But I do not want them

In any home of mine.

Cow-moo-flage

We've all heard of a purple cow

Though no-one's ever seen one.

I'm told that it's more difficult still

To try and spot a green one.

Our Patriarchs

Abraham, Isaac and Jacob

Are honoured and revered.

No doubt, in their time,

They were both loved and feared.

As Old Testament figures

Of fame they have no lack;

But I like to think of them

As Abie, Izzy and Jack.

They led long and eventful lives

Which kept them very busy

Lots of children and many wives

Had Abie, Jack and Izzy.

Their faith in God was boundless.

For them there was no "maybe".

You really have to admire

Izzy, Jack and Abie.

And when, at last, the Messiah comes

I'm sure that they'll be back.

Do you think they'll mind me calling them

Abie, Izzy and Jack?

Laissez Fair?

I'm all for international trade

From major goods to minor,

But most of the things for which I've paid

Now say they're "Made in China".

The Old Fashioned Way

For many years we have been told

That force is not the solution.

Persuasion and diplomacy

Best yield a resolution.

If this philosophy really works

Then why, in biblical times,

Did not Moses return from Mount Sinai

With the ten guidelines?

Desirable Development

The freeway starts at the top of the street,

The railway's behind that old shed,

The subway rumbles beneath your feet,

There's a flight path overhead.

Trucks and buses roar past the gate,

The sports stadium's on the next plot

This has to be the ideal place

To build a parking lot.

Cover up

"I stand for honesty and truth."

That is what he said;

But as everybody knows,

He always lies in bed.

Mentally Challenged

My attention's undivided

My concentration's rapt.

That is, of course, provided

The subject matter's apt.

My attention starts to wander

And my concentration lapses

If there is nothing there to ponder

And the argument collapses.

Consumer complaint

I try to keep a low profile,

Keep myself to myself if I can,

But, although I am one of so many,

There is something wrong with my plan.

I don't want to complete a survey

That is ten pages long and all that.

Who cares if I have won a prize

Should my name be drawn from the hat.

I don't want to buy a magazine,

Nor get double-glazing that's "free".

Please find someone else to pick on

And leave my business to me.

Braggart

"I sleep like a babe," I heard him tell

Now this I'm sure is a lie,

For, if he did, I know full well,

He'd wake each hour and cry.

"I'm fit as a fiddle," he did declare

He really should mind his tongue,

As all the fiddles of which I'm aware

Are very highly strung.

"I eat like a horse," was his final boast

This really is loose talk,

For he'd be famous coast to coast

With a nosebag instead of a fork.

Universal Language

I love space movies,

I'm under their spell,

But how do the aliens

Speak English so well?

Envy

I met a charming fellow

And we had quite a chat.

He said some very clever things.

I wish that I'd said that.

I saw him a few days later,

He'd bought a brand new hat.

It really did look very smart.

I wish that I'd bought that.

He invited me to supper,

To see his Chelsea flat,

With a lovely view across the Thames.

I wish that I had that.

We went to play some cricket,

He's a great one with a bat.

He scored an easy century.

I wish I could do that.

He finished up in prison

In Wormwood Scrubs, he's at.

He stole a lot of money.

I'm pleased I didn't do that.

Could You Do It?

If they gave you a gun to kill, could you do it?

If they gave you a bomb to blow up a bus or a train

And barbed wire to place around men and women

And mines that terrorise and maim

Could you do it?

If they took you away from your wife and children

And gave you a uniform all spick and span

And with it a rifle, a bayonet, a knife

And said the war will make you a man

Could you do it?

If they told you that what you are doing is right

To save the world from evil and terror

That we must fight to save our way of life

And that the enemy is in error

Could you do it?

If you go to war and felt and saw

The death, the suffering and the pain

The broken bodies and shattered minds

And then were asked to fight again

Could you do it?

FANCY TRICKS

Final Resting Place

When father was cremated

They didn't have an urn,

So they put him in a bottle

Which gave us quite a turn.

But the bottle is quite pretty

With a very neat screw top.

We keep it on the sideboard

Labelled "one bottle of pop".

Colour Coordinated

I'm back to wearing fancy ties

With colours bright that fetch up

Those reds and blues and greens and pinks

And gravy stains and ketchup.

Meaty Treaty

A nuclear treaty's been won.

A nuclear ban has begun.

Just as well it applies

To the earth and our skies

And not to the stars and the sun.

The Bucket

I recently bought a bucket,

The plastic type – you know.

I filled it up with water

Then kicked it with my toe.

"Oh God, I've kicked the bucket,"

I said without a thought

But it seems that someone heard me

In a place they shouldn't aught

For a voice came down from heaven

And whispered in my head

"According to our records

You are definitely not dead."

Complicated Arthur

(To be read with a Northern accent)

The trouble with our Arthur is

He makes things complicated.

It's not that he's a genius

Or even highly rated;

But give him a simple job to do

That should only take five secs

Come back an hour later

And he's still working on the specs.

He was like this from an early age,

He weren't like other boys.

Why he could play for days and days

With the simplest of toys.

Don't ask him to hang a picture

Or mend an electric fuse;

He'd take forever doing it

And it still would be no use.

But now he's found his calling

And it makes us truly nervous.

He's gone up to bloody London

And joined the Civil Service.

Middle-Aged Toy

I have a brand new sports car

Complete with every gizmo

I do not drive it very far

But it sure helps my machismo.

See You, EU

Economic co-operation I'm all for.

Free trade and keep open the door.

But bureaucrats in Brussels

Flexing their muscles

Is something that I abhor.

LIMERICKS

There was a chess master of weight

Wed a girl from an alien state.

Now the experts all say

He has ruined his play

By taking a Czech for a mate.

Two grave robbers once from Androsing

To rob Beethoven's grave were proposing.

They lifted the coffin

And took the lid off 'im

And there he still was, decomposing.

A young lady of good disposition

Began to restrict her nutrition,

So from plump and hale

She became thin and pale

And ill-temperedly shot her dietician.

There was a gas fitter from Troon

Who asked an old flame to his room.

This attempt at wooing

Proved his undoing

When his unfitted gas pipe went "Boom!".

"There's a brothel," he said, "that's so green,

They pay you when you've finished your scene."

"That's great. Where's it at?"

"Oh, I'm not sure of that

As, so far, it's the wife that has been."

It's been raining for weeks hereabout

And my brolly is almost worn out

Each time there's a flood

It leaves filth and mud

But next summer, no doubt, we'll have drought.

The giraffe is a strange looking mammal

On a par, perhaps, with the camel;

But it is the ostrich,

That amusing bird, which

Was voted top place by our panel.

A sexy young lady named Mabel

Liked to do it on the dining room table.

Mother asked the maid,

"Has the table been laid?"

But it wasn't the table, it was Mabel.

There was a young lady from Dover

Who had pimples and spots all over

Except in one place

That was not on her face

Known only to her pet dog, Rover.

A portrait they call Mona Lisa

Was done by an Italian geezer

To smile she tried

But she couldn't hide

That nothing he painted would please her.

A young lady whose name was Felicity

Was renowned for her sexual duplicity;

But being well bred

She reserved her bed

For upper crust gents explicitly.

There was a young lady called Anna,

Who had a most charming manner,

All the men who knew her

Tried to woo her,

But she fended them off with a spanner.

There was a young lady called Gina

Who played a small concertina,

And all she would wear

Was a flower in her hair –

I think it was a gardenia.

There was a young lady called Jill

Who decided to come off the pill

She found a mate

To procreate

And I'm told that they're at it still.

There was a young girl from Kilkenny

Whose favours were varied and many

Men would queue

For an hour or two

But some of them never got any.

Milton Keynes UK
Ingram Content Group UK Ltd.
UKHW022315020424
440481UK00015B/595